Copyright ©2019 by EbonyJanice Moore.

Ebony Janice Moore www.ebonyjanice.com

No part of this book may be reproduced or transmitted in any form or by any means electronic, mechanical, including photocopying and recording, or by any information storage or retrieval system, except as may be expressly permitted in writing by the author. All requests should be addressed to EbonyJanice Moore freepeople@thefreepeopleproject.com

Table Of Contents

The Importance of Creating Rituals.....8

Introduction..12

Part 1 Methodology & Pedegogy...........18

Part 2 Mindset..58

Part 3 Strategy & Monday......................98

Part 4 Resources...................................112

Part 5 Journal Pages.............................116

"Saw things I imagined
I saw things I imagined
I saw things I imagined
I saw things I imagined
I saw things I imagined
Things I imagined
Things I imagined
Things I imagined
Saw things I imagined
I saw things I imagined
I saw things I imagined
I saw things I imagined
I saw things I imagined
Things I imagined
Things I imagined
Things I imagined"
- "Saw Things I Imagined"
x Solange Knowles

The Importance of Creating Rituals

I grew up in the black church; which is to say that nothing starts without prayer and devotion of some sort. Devotion usually looks like 1-3 songs, prayer (sometimes praying until tears), and then ending in a song before turning it over to the service or program leader. The prayer is a part of devotion but it's never just a prayer - it's a pleading, a begging, a crying, a conjuring, calling and calling Jesus up and telling him what we want. And what we want is for Him to "come by here" and see about us during this service or ceremony.

Here we are at the introduction of this workbook and

Solange is our Devotion leader. She is the literal "Ritual of Resistance" that we are using to ease ourselves into this learning, growing, and healing experience. She is both the song selection and the prayer; except there is no pleading, begging, crying - solely a conjuring, a calling and calling the Most High inside of ourselves up and telling (Her) waht we want. And what we want is for (Her) to "come by here" and give us the confidence to be who we were called to be during this service and ceremony called "Life."

Rituals are important because they ground us in our practice. When Solange sings, "Saw things I imagined" on repeat, it is an affirmation and a declaration. She understands the power of the scripture that says, "Speak those things that are not as though they were." (Romans 4:17) In order to see the things we imagined we have to give ourselves the permission, space, and time to actually imagine them. Then we need to speak them - just say them out loud until we see what we had previously only saw in our dreams and in our prayers.

Thank you for joining me on this journey to Dream Ourselves Free. I am looking forward to singing, praying, and declaring our way into all the dreaming, playing, and joy that this life has to offer. May these rituals and these words live inside of us with so much ease that we never have to plead, beg, or cry to get the light to show up... it just always was, is, and is to come.

Introduction

Hi. My name is EbonyJanice. I am a preacher, a teacher, and a coach. I came to God through Jesus, have a deep investment in Ancestor reverence and African Spirit Traditions, love and honor the Orisha, and am a Hip Hop Womanist and Theologian. I founded Black Girl Mixtape, a multi-platform lecture series, to be a safe think-space for black women to have their intellectual authority centered. Through Black Girl Mixtape, I teach several courses at BGM Institute and hold space for other educators to share their valuable work and wisdom in that space as well. Additionally, I coach women, most intentionally, black women, into decolonizing authority and doing the work to establish themselves as the expert in their industry.

One day early 2019, I was reading Patrice Kahn Cullors' "When They Call You A Terrorist: A Black Lives Matter Memoir" and she said something about a program she created to be able to support her brother and that triggered something in me that I wanted to start for my nephews. They were 8 and 11 years old at the time, and attending a predominately white school that certainly did not have the tools or the capacity to keep them safe in their learning environment. As I thought about the way I wanted to support my baby nephews, something came over me and I thought, "Absolutely not! I don't have time to create that right now."

I thought about the fact that most people have no clue that Patrice Kahn Cullors is an artist because they only know her through her revolutionary Black Lives Matter work and education. I think that's unfair and I can't fathom that anyone else believes its fair that people in marginalized identities, especially black women, have to create everything from resistance.

Everything.

That's not a metaphor for something... when I say everything, I mean that literally. In order to survive black people (women) have had to be creative, innovative, and resourceful with little to no resources JUST to get by. But what happens when we don't want to just "get by" any more? What happens when you want to thrive? What happens when you just want to enjoy your life and not always have to create something or some organization or some curriculum or some program... just to be safe? Just to have the same basic guarantees as other women? Just to have the same basic opportunities as other human beings?

So that's where Dream Yourself Free, the workshop and now this workbook, came from. I wondered, "Who would black women be if we could create from ease, play, and joy instead of always from resistance?" Would we still be doing what we're currently doing? No matter how amazing we may be at what we do and what we create, would we still be doing "this?" I started asking this question to many brilliant black women who are at the top of their respective industry and 99.9% of them said they would not be doing what they are currently doing. Can you fathom being at the top of your industry and not fully actualized because you're mostly only doing that work for survival? Can you fathom the kind of artist Patrice Kahn Cullor's might be if she didn't have to be marching, organizing, and building an organization that is making, seemingly, a very basic humane statement: Black. Lives. Matter.

I want to live in that world; the world where the most respected activists and community organizers get to put down their picket signs and be celebrated for the brilliance, capacity, and talent that they very rarely get to cultivate and be honored for because they're too busy trying to push programs and policy that simply keep us alive.

Yes, Black Lives Matter - but the WHOLE life matters. Not just the body, the spirt, and the soul as well. Dream Yourself Free is giving us space and tools to begin to put energy and emphasis on that reality.

I'm honored to be on this journey together.

- EbonyJanice

Part 1: Methodology & Pedagogy

Methodology

Growing In Community

- This work is rooted in the idea that the way we grow deeper is to grow together.

Collaborative Coaching

- The work in this workbook was workshopped over a course of several months with 60+ brilliant black women that supported each other in their development and simultaneously helped me to get even more clear about the ways we heal and grow together.

Co-creating Knowledge

- When people get together and have conversations on a specific topic, whatever we discuss in that space becomes a collaborative learning effort. We, literally, create knowledge together.

Decolonized Healing

- A colonized healing practice suggests that there is only one, westernized, way to heal. Decolonized Healing trusts that there are other modalities of healing. This workshop-turned-workbook is one such way that we heal ourselves in a way that assumes our joy is a central part of our healing.

Pedagogy: Black women's ease for dreaming

I wrote a play years ago called, "Before: When We Were Beautiful…" it was a conversation on black women being stripped of their ability to be "beautiful" on the transatlantic slave trade journey. It started with a conversation I was having with a man in my early twenties where he called me "beautiful" and I realized I was use to being "sexy" but had rarely been given permission, at that point in my life, to be beautiful - or even pretty… always sexy… never just pretty/beautiful. There was some internal conflict about the idea of my body having been sexualized before I knew anything about what sex or sensuality even was. Who are we if our beauty is unacceptable while simultaneously being "all the rage?"

"What do you do if you don't have beauty?" "Who are we without our beauty?" "What is joy without the feeling of beauty?" "Where is pleasure without the affirmation of beauty?" Even our sacred text (the Bible) tells us that beauty is "fleeting" but in what ways has black women's beauty been policed in even more harmful ways than other groups of people as a result of intentional invisibilization and also as a result of our bodies being the only human bodies being used for both reproduction and labor (as a result of chattel slavery)?

But, I'm thinking about a conversation I had with artist, therapist, and free girl, Thea Monyee when she said, "I am OWED decades worth of pleasure" and I had to take a moment to pause to say, "OWED!" I had to really let that word linger on my tongue, swish over the roof of my mouth, sit for a moment in the air and feel what it felt like to think about the fact that I am OWED (meaning I am due) some pleasure. As in, "somebody need to run me my pleasure!"

Who would we be if our organizing, justice pursuit, and mission/ministry was about our self pleasure, FIRST, and everything else after? We always hear that we are supposed to pour from a full cup or the idea that if we are on a plane and the oxygen masks drop we are to put our own masks on first then help others. However, that is not the reality black women have been living with and this work is about undoing the discomfort we feel around beauty, pleasure, and self care as a radical act of reverence and worship.

Purpose: To explore how to increase black women's capacity to create their purpose driven lives from a place of ease through dreaming and playing.

Who are you?

Name?

If you could do X today what would it be?

What is the last thing you did that was play?

What are you currently anticipating?

If there were no limits or boundaries what would your life look like on a daily basis?

If there were no limits or boundaries what would your relationships look like on a daily basis?

Do you have self care rituals?

List them:

If there were no limits or boundaries what would your self care rituals look like on a daily basis?

A Reading:

"When warm weather came, Baby Suggs, holy, followed by every black man, woman, and child who could make it through, took her great heart to the Clearing--a wide-open place cut deep in the woods nobody knew for what at the end of the path known only to deer and whoever cleared the land in the first place. In the heat of every Saturday afternoon, she sat in the clearing while the people waited among the trees.

After situating herself on a huge flat-sided rock, Baby Suggs bowed her head and prayed silently. The company watched her from the trees. They knew she was ready when she put her stick down. Then she shouted, 'Let the children come!' and they ran from the trees toward her.

Let your mothers hear you laugh,' she told them, and the woods rang. The adults looked on and could not help smiling.

Then 'Let the grown men come,' she shouted. They stepped out one by one from among the ringing trees.

Let your wives and your children see you dance,' she told them, and ground life shuddered under their feet.

Finally she called the women to her. 'Cry,' she told them. 'For the living and the dead. Just cry.' And without covering their eyes the women let loose.

It started that way: laughing children, dancing men, crying women and then it got mixed up. Women stopped crying and danced; men sat down and cried; children danced, women laughed, children cried until, exhausted and riven, all and each lay about the Clearing damp and gasping for breath. In the silence that followed, Baby Suggs, holy, offered up to them her great big heart.

She did not tell them to clean up their lives or go and sin no more. She did not tell them they were the blessed of the earth, its inheriting meek or its glorybound pure.

She told them that the only grace they could have was the grace they could imagine. That if they could not see it, they would not have it.

Here,' she said, 'in this here place, we flesh; flesh that weeps, laughs; flesh that dances on bare feet in grass. Love it. Love it hard..."

What comes up for you while reading that?

How does it make you feel?

What does the visual of the dancing, crying, laughing mean for you?

When Baby Suggs talks about "flesh" as a verb, what does this make you think?

When is the last time you laughed until you felt whole?

When is the last time you cried until you felt whole?

When is the last time you danced until you felt whole?

What other actions make you feel whole?

When is the last time you did any of those actions until you felt whole?

Afrofuturism is a cultural aesthetic, philosophy of science, and philosophy of history that explores the developing intersection of African Diaspora culture with technology. It is the prophesy of blackness in the future. In this work, we will explore an afrofuturistic methodology where we envision the black women in the future as the most actualized, free, and full of joy versions of themselves.

Why does this matter if you are not a black woman?

Do you understand that black women live in a very unique intersection of marginalized identities; gender and race. As a result: "When black women are free everyone will be free." - The Combahee River Collective

What is the afrofuture of black women's ease?

What does heaven look like for black women?

*If you are nonblack doing this work, what does it look like for you whole and holy to live into an Afrofuturistic reality where black women's ease is a given and an essential part of the human existence?

- What does your personal religious/spiritual truth system suggest to you about caring for yourself, experiencing ease, and enjoying play and dreaming?

We have heard the saying, "I am my ancestors wildest imagination." While I believe that it is very presumptuous to assume that we are the best that our ancestors could imagine, I do think that using our prayers, meditation, and imagination to consider the highest thoughts of our ancestors to guide us onward into our most beautiful future is wisdom and might reveal the ways we should maneuver in various situations that help us find joy and play.

Think of a situation that you are currently working through. What would your most honorable ancestors say about the situation?

If the goal is to create from ease instead of from resistance it may be important for us to stop centering whiteness in everything we do. Here's a thing to consider about one of our most honorable ancestors: "Harriet Tubman wasn't fighting white people she was just focused on freedom." Use the space below to journal your response to this truth. How does this knowing inspire you in your current work where you may have been previously centering whiteness (even your own proximity to whiteness or your own whiteness if you are a nonblack or nonPOC accessing this work)?

"My world is a black world, the white world is just peripheral." - Toni Morrison

How much of your current existence is framed by or centers whiteness? Be honest about how that is impacting your current existence (including your mental, spiritual, and physical wellbeing).

What does it mean to create structures and support systems towards a financially sustainability for black women's dreaming/ease?

- What models exist? (Who are the free black girls that we know and why do we consider them free?) (A few examples: Girl Trek, Beyonce, Solange, Janelle Monae, Oprah) Use the space below to write down more free black girl images and journal about "why" we consider them free. This activity is important because it will help us to build upon our truth that financial sustainability as a free black woman is possible.

"I'm weary of the ways of the world

Be weary of the ways of the world

I'm weary of the ways of the world

I'm going look for my body yeah

I'll be back real soon

You going look for my body yeah

I'll be back real soon

I'm going look for my body yeah

I'll be back real soon"

- Weary x Solange Knowles

How does Solange go from Weary of the Ways of the world to Saw things I imagined? I wanted to think about this because as we transition in this workbook from our imagination to a more strategy based creative process, it's important to me that we have some details and specifics about how someone could go from a heavy laden lamentation about what it feels like to be in this black femme body to the celebration of all the things blackness and woman in the very next creative project they release a few short years later.

What are some things we can use our imagination to believe she did to heal herself from weary of the ways of the world to saw things I imagined?

(Fasted? Watched Lemonade? Therapy? Get a coach? Detox? Walk? Balance her chakras?)

Imagine together (Let's cocreate a dream world where black women can create from ease - what does that place look like, who is there, who isn't there, what's good, whats the weather, what is happening? Why are we free there? What are the things we can do (collectively and individually) Today to make this a reality for us? What does play and ease look like in this place?

- Black women are seen
- We laugh until we cry. Often.
- We are the standard and aren't criticized for our contribution to society while other folk are celebrated for what they appropriated from us.
- We breathe ease.
- We receive help without having to ask for it.

Read 2 Kings 4:1-7 in the Bible.

This woman said "all i have is some oil." "All I have..." but really that was poverty mindset speaking because it shows how much she undervalued that oil. She didn't think what she had was good enough or that it could support her. We tend to create from this very same place of lack. We make "all I have..." confessions on a regular basis because we can't fathom that "all I have" is overflow and abundant! This is the mindset shift work that we need to do to shift from our lack to our abundance mindset. Understand that she didn't actually end up creating from lack... She created from "what do you have" --- she saw it as a little but it was literally wealth in her house right then and there.

Assignment:

Go to that free black woman afro futuristic space that we just cocreated together. Close your eyes. Deep breaths. Exhale deeply. Imagine yourself as a little child. Who do you want to be when you grow up and get to exist in this afro futuristic black femme liberated space? What is the highest version of yourself from that free, informed, empowered place?

Part 2: Mindset

I need to tell you a quick story. In 2016 I came across this IG account of this woman that I thought was beautiful but extremely annoying. She wasn't doing anything, in particular, that was actually annoying - just living her life. It irked me like no other for some reason. So I would scroll past her anytime someone posted or reposted something about her. At the same time, I had been processing all the things I've been telling you about in this book. I needed my coaching clients to be better and to be changed forever by our work together, therefore I needed to be better and changed forever. I knew that if I was going to make the kind of impact on their lives that I wanted to make - then I needed to be a better, higher, more authentic version of myself.

That's where this woman on IG came in. I LOVE black women and I have created an entire platform around celebrating black women so this really bothered me that I was this bothered by this beautiful black woman just minding her business. I finally realized I was envious of her freedom. I realized that I needed to learn something from her. So I started following her on all social media platforms and she talked a lot about meditation and spiritual growth and how THAT is what brought her into this free place. She talked about how meditation helped her begin to heal from insecurity, depression, and the paralyzing fear that was keeping her from becoming who she wanted to be. And how this internal work helped her begin to create a new life for herself - the life she actually wanted to live.

I wanted that. But I knew it wasn't going to happen overnight.

And I knew it was going to take more than JUST meditation.

So I went on a journey to discovering HOW to become the person I really wanted to be...

So that my work could impact people in a more lasting and meaningful way!

I read 100's of books and listened to 100's of hours worth of audio PLUS I started coaching more intentionally with my own coach & even paid for additional training & mentoring.

Everybody had a few things in common and since *success leaves clues* I decided to focus my energy on what I call "The Power Tools" that pretty much all successful people use to live their best lives!

THESE ARE THE

4 POWER TOOLS

THAT WILL

DRASTICALLY

CHANGE YOUR

LIFE FROM

DAY TO DAY

1. Meditation

I talk about meditation as a powerful life-altering tool in my book, "Five Miles to Jesus: The Radical Worship That Saved My Life"

If you haven't read my book yet, for some strange reason - let me add that meditation isn't just a woo woo idea. It is scientifically proven that meditation can shift your entire being.

  - "MRI scans show that after an eight-week

course of mindfulness practice, the brain's "fight or flight" center, the amygdala, appears to shrink. This primal region of the brain, associated with fear and emotion, is involved in the initiation of the body's response to stress."

- The relaxation response [from meditation] helps decrease metabolism, lowers blood pressure, and improves heart rate, breathing, and brain waves. Tension and tightness seep from muscles as the body receives a quiet message to relax."

- Meditation has been linked to a number of things that lead to increased ability to focus, memory, and concentration.

Can we talk about LL Cool J for a second?

I once heard LL Cool J say that people would rather believe he has had plastic surgery on his body to look the way he looks than believe he does what he does to look the way he looks.

Same goes for these "Power Tools"

I know you are here because you want the strategy it takes to take your life to the next level so when I say something like, "Meditation is a POWER TOOL that you MUST use to realize great success - you want to be like, "Okay girl! Where is the log off button?"

One way that meditation has been POWERFUL in changing my life and taking my career, my finances, my relationships, and my dream projects to the next level is that meditating FIRST thing in the morning ensures that I enter the day as my whole self.

Not with the residue of

yesterday on me.

Not with the anxiety of

tomorrow on me.

But as a fully grounded,

sharper thinking, equipped,

and focused person with a clear

mission.

What does the fully grounded,

sharper thinking, equipped,

and focused version of your life

look like?

What Does My Meditation Practice Look Like?

- Prayer

- Altar Work

- Balancing my chakras (You can use youtube meditations)

- Deep breathing

- Paying attention to your body/needs

What Does Your Meditation Practice Look Like?

2. Affirmations

We can adopt healthy, positive, and productive beliefs if we recite a belief enough times to ourselves.

Do you understand why this is so important to your personal development and your success?

...because you have whatever you believe.

[What do you currently believe about your health, wellness, finances, dream projects, relationships? How is that showing up in your life?]

Here's a perfect example of how I use affirmations in EVERY area of my life:

The affirmation that I say to myself more than ANY other affirmation is:

"Everything is going smooth and easy."

I say it when I'm walking into Starbucks and need a table next to an outlet.

I say it when I'm pulling into a crowded parking lot and need to find a space with great ease.

I say it at the airport when I'm checking in and going through TSA (often in a rush).

"Everything is going smooth and easy for me."

I say this so much that it's not something I HOPE - it has literally become my TRUTH!

"Everything is going smooth and easy for me" is now part of my life's truth bank and because I believe that internally as an actual and factual reality...
EVERYTHING goes smooth and easy for me... especially

when I really need that to

kick in and be TRUTH!

What about when it doesn't turn out how I expected it to turn out?

When it doesn't turn out the way I expected it to turn out then I employ meditation and affirmations TOGETHER as a combination work to keep me grounded, focused, clear on my intention and desire, and available for whatever is happening enough to be able to PERCEIVE the deeper meaning or the larger lesson. When I consider these affirmations and this truth. everything is STILL going smooth and easy for me even if it doesn't work out the way I thought it should work out.

When is the last time something did not go the way you thought it should go but it turned out to be in your favor anyways?

3. Visualization

According to research using brain imagery, visualization works because neurons in our brains, those electrically excitable cells that transmit information, interpret imagery as equivalent to a real-life action. When we visualize an act, the brain generates an impulse that tells our neurons to "perform" the movement.

Roger Bannister, the first person to ever run a 4 minute mile said he was able to do it because "I spent hours practicing, planning, strategizing, and visualizing himself running that mile in 4 minutes."

Positive thinking isn't enough, but it creates a mindset that allows the intersection of superior planning and execution.

Ambitious beliefs lead to ambitious goals. Limiting beliefs lead to impotent goals. You will rarely accomplish more than what you set out to, and can't hit the target if you're not aiming for it and "You will only reach for what you have seen." - Michelle Obama

Or... in the words of Karen Clark Sheard, "You gotta see it, before you see it, or you never will see it!"

Let me tell you a quick story about how visualization helped me save $1000's of dollars in refunds a few summers ago...

Erykah Badu reposted my WWEB bodysuit.

The sale was still in preorder and I had only prepared for MAX 100 orders. MAX! But I ended up getting near 350 preorders overnight after she posted.

I was STRESSED!

1st the Wholesalers ran out of Red bodysuits.

Then my designs weren't staying on the bodysuits.

I was going to have to refund EVERYONE.

Something said, "Visualize yourself solving this problem with great ease."

TRUE STORY: I started visualizing myself solving each problem and INSTANTLY I downloaded solutions for both problems with GREAT ease.

That showed me that not only is visualization a tangible tool for seeing yourself accomplishing something you've set out to accomplish but it's also a BRILLIANT tool for accomplishing what you don't even know you know HOW to accomplish. The answers really do be within.

4. Morning Pages

THISSSSSSSS!

Aside from drastic improvements to your mood and emotional well-being, writing out your thoughts and feelings regularly can actually benefit your physical health as well. Journaling can increase your chance of fighting specific diseases like asthma, rheumatoid arthritis, AIDS and cancer. Amazingly, it can even help physical wounds heal faster.

A study conducted in 2013 found that 76% of adults who spent 20 minutes a day journaling for three days in a row before a scheduled medical biopsy were fully healed 11 days later. On the other hand, 58% of the control group had not yet recovered. The study concluded that just one hour of writing about a distressing event helped the participants to better understand the events and reduce stress levels.

So with that - understand that STARTING your day writing in a journal has SCIENTIFICALLY proven to be beneficial MIND|

Body|&SOUL

Do you have goals?

Have you written them down some place?

    Daily goals?

    Where are they listed?

    When do you check in on them?

WEEKLY GOALS?

How do you know if you're making progress on them?

2018

YEAR GOALS?

WHERE THEY AT THO?

Part 3: Strategy

& Money

Choose a Project/Goal/Book/Thing To Launch

- What is it?

- What is the intention? (What do you want it to do for the world? Your community? Your career? Your family?)

- Why is it?

- Whats the timeframe? (specific date)

Brain dump:

List all the things you think you'd need to do to begin, continue, remain, produce, launch? Every single thing.

After this list is done, I will explain how to take this list and turn it into a real life thing. You also must schedule in having intentional fun (an artist date) on each week the agenda you're about to create.

Now that you have brain dumped every thing you need to do to move forward towards the goal of releasing, launching, or producing your thing - take everything on the list and put it on individual sticky notes or notecards.

Next, take those individual sticky notes or note cards and put them in order of priority to in the future... Priority things can be done today through this week. In the future could be considered next week to next month.

Now that you have put everything in order you should take the action items and put them on your calendar. Don't forget to schedule in time for rest, creativity, play, and enjoying the process.

Question: What things will you do to celebrate yourself as you accomplish the action items that are now scheduled (date and time) in your calendar?

Think of 2 King 4:1-7 and write down what do you have in your house? What is your current oil?

What is coming up for you around self esteem, worth, and lack?

What do you have versus what you **think** you need to even begin?

Charging

Your Money blueprint is how you have been programmed to respond to money and wealth throughout your life, beginning in your childhood.

(i.e. If your father told you "Money doesn't grow on trees" you may have a hard time imagining that money comes to you with ease. If your mother told you that "People with a lot of money are evil, stingy, and corrupt you may have a hard time holding on to money because you subconsciously believe that having money makes you evil.)

What statements have contributed to your money blueprint?

What affirmations and new stories could you create and affirm to replace some of the limiting beliefs you just identified you have about money?

What does the following phrase bring to your mind? Journal your thoughts:

If I charged like a below average, overly confident white man, I would charge

_____ for this product/service.

Here's a reminder: Stop counting people's money inside their pockets. This means you have been giving discounts based on what you think people can afford rather than the value you add. Stop giving discounts because you assume someone can't afford

to pay you what you are worth.

Part 4: Resources

Black Joy Zine (Published by Sanaa Carats) http://www.magcloud.com/browse/issue/1622506

What's In Your Heart Coloring Journal: A Therapeutic Journaling Experience by Danee K. Black www.whatsinyourheart.bigcartel.com

Curvy Curly Conscious' "PlayShop" with Shelah Marie www.curvycurlyconscious.com

The Black Joy Project https://www.instagram.com/theblackjoyproject/

Black Joy Parade 2020 www.blackjoyparade.org

Cuz I Love You (album) by Lizzo

Alone At Last (album) by Tasha (emphasis on "Lullaby" song)

The Free People ^ Church Project by EbonyJanice www.thefreepeopleproject.com

Black Girl Mixtape (Podcast) www.blackgirlmistape.com

The Artist's Way by Julia Cameron

Part 5: Journal Pages

Made in the USA
Middletown, DE
11 January 2021